Everyday Heroes

The
National Guard

Nichol Bryan
ABDO Publishing Company

visit us at
www.abdopub.com

Published by ABDO Publishing Company, 4940 Viking Drive, Edina, Minnesota 55435.
Copyright © 2003 by Abdo Consulting Group, Inc. International copyrights reserved in all
countries. No part of this book may be reproduced in any form without written permission from
the publisher.

Printed in the United States.

Editors: Kate A. Conley, Stephanie Hedlund, Kristianne E. Vieregger
Photo Credits: Corbis
Art Direction: Neil Klinepier

Library of Congress Cataloging-in-Publication Data

Bryan, Nichol, 1958-
   The National Guard / Nichol Bryan.
     p. cm. -- (Everyday heroes)
   Includes index.
   Summary: Describes the history, role, training, and duties of the United States National Guard.
   ISBN 1-57765-858-2
    1. United States--National Guard--Juvenile literature. [1. United States--National
Guard. 2. Occupations.] I. Title. II. Everyday heroes (Edina, Minn.)

UA42.B78 2002
355.3'7'0973--dc21

                            2002066665

Contents

The National Guard

You've probably seen soldiers on television or in movies. But did you know that some soldiers might live right in your community? You may even know some of them, but you might not realize they're soldiers! They are members of the National Guard.

The National Guard is a special force of citizen soldiers. Most of the time, their lives are much like those of other people. They go to their jobs and live at home with their families.

But during emergencies, members of the National Guard are called to action. They help the regular army and air force fight in the country's wars. And they help during natural **disasters** such as floods, fires, and earthquakes.

This National Guard member could live in your community!

National Guard members do all sorts of jobs. And they use all kinds of equipment. They train regularly to protect their country and community. At a moment's notice, these men and women are ready to turn into soldiers.

National Guard members in uniform

History of the National Guard

The National Guard is the oldest part of the U.S. armed forces. Even before the United States was founded, people volunteered to guard their communities from attack. These groups of volunteers were called **militias**.

The first militia in the U.S. colonies was formed in 1607. As the colonies grew, their militias became more organized. By 1636, these groups were protecting colonists against Native American **raids**.

When the colonies fought to be free from Britain, militia groups did most of the fighting. General George Washington relied on farmers and townspeople who volunteered. After a battle, these volunteers were free to go back to their homes. Even after the United States won its freedom, it relied on militias to defend the country.

The National Guard
Through the Years

1861

1967

1992

2001

In the 1800s, many state **militias** called themselves National Guards. Then, in 1903, the U.S. **Congress** passed a law that united all of the state militias into a single fighting force. The law officially named this new force the National Guard. But it is commonly called the guard.

An Observation Squadron in 1929

The guard has fought in every U.S. war. When the United States started to use airplanes during **World War I**, pilots were forced to leave the guard. They formed special flying squads called Observation Squadrons.

After **World War II**, these squads were joined. They formed a new fighting force called the Air National Guard. So now the National Guard has two parts, the Army National Guard and the Air National Guard.

The F-16A Falcon is an aircraft used by today's Air National Guard. It can carry bombs, missiles, and a cannon.

Today, the National Guard has more than 400,000 members. Its role in the nation's defense is more important than ever. The United States relies on the guard to fight when the country needs it.

Guard Funding

Keeping a large, full-time army is expensive. So the U.S. government keeps a smaller, regular army. This means the government relies on guard members during **disasters**, wars, and emergencies.

The money to run the guard comes from the federal government and the individual states. The federal government provides the money to pay the people in the guard. It also pays for the guard's tanks, aircraft, and other equipment.

John Brown's Fort is part of the armory in Harpers Ferry, West Virginia.

The states must pay for their own armories. Armories are the buildings where guard members train each month and store their equipment. There are more than 3,200 guard armories in the United States.

Both the state and the federal government run the guard. In times of peace, each state's National Guard is under the command of its governor. The governor can call on the guard to help in events such as natural **disasters** or **riots**. During war, the president can place the guard in the command of the regular armed forces.

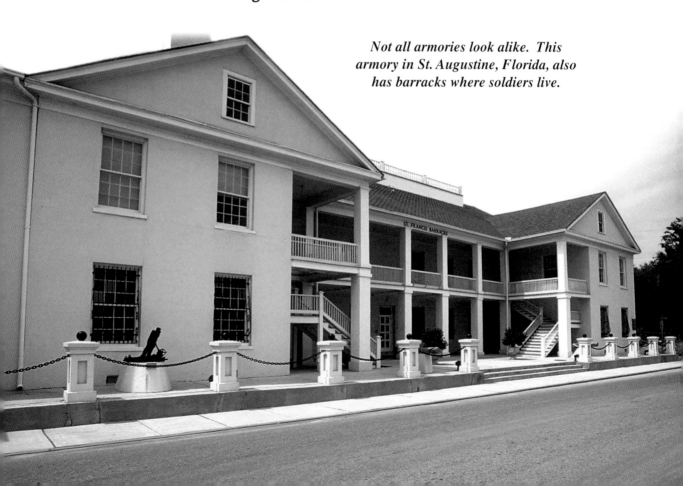

Not all armories look alike. This armory in St. Augustine, Florida, also has barracks where soldiers live.

What They Do

The National Guard has three basic duties. It serves as a reserve that helps the armed forces in times of war. It provides emergency relief during **disasters**. And it works to preserve peace and public order.

Guard members can have many different jobs. Some fly combat jets, or operate tanks on the battlefield. Some transport food, weapons, and supplies. Others provide medical help. Still others perform police duties, or gather information on the enemy.

The guard helped remove snow when Buffalo, New York, was covered with two feet (61 cm) during one storm in November 2000.

During war, guard units serve in every part of combat. In the **Vietnam War**, guard units served as rangers. They patrolled the jungle and **raided** enemy posts. In **Operation Desert Storm**, Army National Guard units launched rockets into Iraq. In addition, Air National Guard missions kept the Iraqi air force on the ground.

National Guard members are often called to help with sandbagging when flooding occurs.

Guard members are also ready to help in emergencies at home. When Hurricane Andrew hit Florida in 1992, the National Guard rescued people. They also gave victims food and shelter. When floods struck the Midwest in 1993, the guard helped, too. They built walls to keep back the water and moved people out of danger.

After the **terrorist** attacks on September 11, 2001, guard units helped again. They cleared away the ruins of the World Trade Center. And they dug through the debris looking for survivors.

The guard also plays a police role. When protesters in Seattle, Washington, became violent in 1999, guard units helped keep order. They patrolled the 2002 Winter Olympic Games in Salt Lake City, Utah. And guard units have been sent to keep peace in places such as Somalia, Kosovo, and Haiti.

In addition, guard members have many other duties. Some are trained to stop illegal drugs from entering the country. Some receive special counter-terrorism training.

Opposite page: Soldiers are also called on to perform police duties. This unit is guarding a building in Kosovo during a peacekeeping mission in 2000.

They learn how to spot possible **terrorist** threats and protect people from them.

After September 11, 2001, the National Guard had new jobs. Members of the Air National Guard flew patrols over U.S. cities. The Army National Guard went to more than 400 of the nation's largest airports. They set up security checkpoints to prevent weapons from getting on airplanes.

Guard Requirements

To join the National Guard, you have to meet many requirements. You must be between the ages 17 and 35 and have a high school diploma. You also need to be in good health and not have a serious physical handicap. And you need to take a special test. The test shows if you have the knowledge to succeed in the guard.

Guard members must attend basic training. Basic training is a tough, six- to nine-week training program. Guard members exercise and run many miles to get into great physical shape. They learn all the skills soldiers need in the field. They also learn how to salute, march, and fire a rifle.

After basic training, guard members must serve 12 weeks of **technical** training with the regular

All members of the military attend the same basic training. This makes it easier for them to work together during a crisis.

armed forces. They have the same duties as regular soldiers but also learn specific jobs. When their 12 weeks are up, they go back to their homes.

Guard members serve from three to eight years. During this time, they must train for one weekend each month. They also train for two weeks during the summer.

Guard members endure tough physical and mental training!

A Day in the Guard

Most days, a guard member's life is much like anyone else's. That's because guard members work at regular jobs. They may be factory workers, business executives, doctors, or teachers.

But guard members must be ready to act quickly. Families need to understand that guard members might suddenly be called away. They may be gone for hours, days, or even months.

Guard members must leave their families and jobs to attend the required training. During these training periods, they may live at their armory. They wear combat uniforms and perform their military jobs.

While at training, guard members improve their skills. They practice firing weapons and maintain their good physical shape. They operate and repair the equipment, **vehicles**, and aircraft they use. Guard members also practice the job they learned after basic training and learn new skills. This regular training means the National Guard is always ready to go into action.

National Guard members may be called away at any time. It is hard for them to say good-bye to their families, but they are proud to be of service to their country.

During emergencies, National Guard members can face all kinds of challenges. Guard members go into areas struck by earthquakes, floods, fires, and storms to rescue people. Some guard members give medical aid to soldiers on the battlefield. When helping the police, they risk becoming the victims of violence themselves.

Despite the risks, guard members are proud of the job they do. They feel pride in their 400-year history of protecting and helping our country. And they feel good knowing that when situations are most desperate, they are the ones the nation relies on.

National Guard members receive other benefits as well. They get paid for the times they are in training and in active service. People can get money for college when they join the guard after high school. And guard members receive a lot of special training. This can help them get good jobs in **civilian** life.

Opposite page: President George W. Bush shakes hands with National Guard troops. He visited the West Virginia National Guard Headquarters in Charleston, West Virginia, on February 14, 2001.

Tools of the Guard

Guard members learn to use many kinds of equipment. Because they are soldiers, they learn to use weapons. They practice **marksmanship** with guns like the M-9 pistol and the M-16 rifle. They spend many hours on the firing range to become expert shots.

Guard members also operate fighting **vehicles**. For instance, they fly Apache **helicopters**. Apaches are fast aircraft that can fire bullets, rockets, and guided **missiles**. M1 tanks are the guard's main battle tanks. They have laser-guided cannons that can shoot shells **accurately**. M1s also have heavy armor to protect the crew during attacks.

The Air National Guard flies many kinds of aircraft. The F-15 Eagle fighter jet can fly at more than twice the speed of sound. It has high-tech systems that let one pilot control the jet and fire **missiles** and explosive shells. The C-5 Galaxy is one of the world's biggest planes. It can carry supplies, **vehicles**, and even whole bridges. It can lift about 270,000 pounds (122,470 kg) of freight!

Guard members train with the M-16 rifle to improve their marksmanship.

National Guard members use other kinds of **vehicles**, too. A construction vehicle called the SEE has a backhoe and a bucket loader. It helps guard members clear debris, level roads, and lift heavy items.

The guard also has the famous HMMWV, or Humvee. This jeep-like vehicle can drive in almost any condition. It can be set up to carry troops or launch **missiles**. The Humvee can carry **portable** shelters or even serve as an **ambulance**.

The guard uses many kinds of high-tech equipment for communicating. Guard members operate **satellite** dishes, **microwave transmitters**, and computer networks. These systems help the guard communicate when in a battle or when phone lines are out. The guard also uses electronic warfare devices. These tools help keep the enemy from communicating.

Computer systems are important tools of the National Guard. They can be used for training, positioning troops, or locating the enemy.

The Guard & You

National Guard members live, work, and attend school right where they serve. So the guard is an everyday part of the towns and cities where its members live.

Usually, people notice the guard when it is on emergency duty. Then the community is grateful for the food, shelter, and security the guard provides. But even when there's no emergency, guard members play an important role in their community.

Many guard units have programs to help neighborhood children. The guard helps Little League programs. It also promotes Boy Scout and Girl Scout activities. Guard members invite children to visit them on Armory Days. They run many other programs for students and other groups in the community. National Guard members try to be good **role models** for young people.

National Guard members encourage Boy and Girl Scout troops. These troop members are honoring their National Guard by visiting a veterans' national cemetery near Los Angeles, California.

Staying Safe

You may never actually see a guard unit in action. If you do, it will most likely be during an emergency or natural **disaster**. During these times, everyone can help the National Guard by being prepared. Here are some tips for staying safe during a disaster or emergency:

- Prepare your home for a natural disaster. Contact your local Federal Emergency Management Agency (FEMA) office to get tips for protection against natural disasters.

- Keep a disaster supply kit at home. The kit should include clean drinking water, flashlights, and canned and dry foods. It should also have a first aid kit to use if someone is hurt.

- Keep a battery-powered radio that can monitor emergency weather forecasts.

- Stay close to your parents, teachers, or other responsible adults.

Develop a **disaster** plan with your family. It should include where to go, who to call, and what you should do during a disaster.

With a disaster plan, you and your family will be prepared if an emergency or disaster occurs.

Glossary

accurate - free of errors.

ambulance - a vehicle that carries sick or injured people.

civilian - not part of the armed forces.

Congress - the lawmaking body of the United States. It is made up of the Senate and the House of Representatives.

disaster - an event that causes suffering or loss of life. Natural disasters include events such as hurricanes, tornadoes, and earthquakes.

helicopter - an aircraft without wings that is lifted from the ground and kept in the air by horizontal propellers.

marksmanship - the skill of accurately shooting at a target.

microwave transmitter - a machine that sends and receives electromagnetic waves. Microwave transmitters are often used in surveillance.

militia - a group of citizens trained for war or emergencies.

missile - a weapon that is thrown or projected to hit a target.

Operation Desert Storm - January 16, 1991, to February 28, 1991. A war in the Persian Gulf to liberate Kuwait from Iraqi forces. It is also known as the Gulf War.

portable - able to be carried or moved.

raid - a sudden attack.

riot - a violent public disorder.

role model - a person whose behavior is imitated by others.

satellite - a man-made object shot into orbit by a rocket.

technical - of or relating to a kind of art, science, profession, or other field.

terrorism - the use of terror, violence, or threats to frighten people into action. A person who does this is a terrorist. Actions taken to fight against terrorism are called counter-terrorism.

vehicle - any device used for carrying persons or objects.

Vietnam War - 1955 to 1975. A long, failed attempt by the United States to stop North Vietnam from taking over South Vietnam.

World War I - 1914 to 1918, fought in Europe. The United States, Great Britain, France, Russia, and their allies were on one side. Germany, Austria-Hungary, and their allies were on the other side. The war began when Archduke Ferdinand of Austria was assassinated. America joined the war in 1917 because Germany began attacking ships that weren't involved in the war.

World War II - 1939 to 1945, fought in Europe, Asia, and Africa. The United States, France, Great Britain, the Soviet Union, and their allies were on one side. Germany, Italy, Japan, and their allies were on the other side. The war began when Germany invaded Poland. The United States entered the war in 1941 after Japan bombed Pearl Harbor, Hawaii.

Web Sites

Would you like to learn more about the National Guard? Please visit **www.abdopub.com** to find up-to-date Web site links about the National Guard and its duties. These links are routinely monitored and updated to provide the most current information available.

Index